I Wonder Why

Zips Have Teeth

and Other Questions About Inventions

Barbara Taylor

Kingfisher

KINGFISHER
An imprint of Larousse plc
Elsley House, 24-30 Great Titchfield Street
London, W1P 7AD

First published by Kingfisher 1996
(hb) 10 9 8 7 6 5 4 3 2 1
(pb) 10 9 8 7 6 5 4 3 2
Copyright © Larousse plc 1996

A CIP catalogue record for this book
is available from the British Library

ISBN 1 85697 412 X (hb)
      1 85697 330 1 (pb)

Phototypeset by Tradespools Ltd, Frome, Somerset
Printed and bound in Italy

Series editor: Clare Oliver
Series designer: David West Children's Books
Author: Barbara Taylor
Consultant: Eryl Davies
Editor: Claire Llewellyn
Art editor: Christina Fraser
Picture researcher: Amanda Francis
Illustrations: Susanna Addario 28-29; Peter Dennis (Linda
    Rogers) 10-11, 18-19; Chris Forsey cover, 22tl, 26tl,
    30-31; Terry Gabbey (AFA Ltd) 20-21; Ruby Green
    14-15, 26-27; Nick Harris (Virgil Pomfret) 24-25; Biz
    Hull (Artist Partners) 4-5, 16-17, 22-23; Tony Kenyon
    (BL Kearley) all cartoons; Nicki Palin 6-7, 8-9, 12-13.

Please note: because of the young reading level
of this book, trademarked names only
carry a trademark symbol in
the index.

CONTENTS

Why do people invent things?

Inventors try to solve problems. They think about people's needs, and come up with an answer. When an inventor noticed how inconvenient big umbrellas were, he invented a folding one that would fit in a bag.

Gone to buy some glue!

● Post-it notes were invented by accident when someone made a glue that didn't stick properly. You could stick down a piece of paper, peel it off, and then re-stick it!

● From the moment you wake up you're surrounded by inventions. Pillows, light bulbs, and even cornflakes all help to give us an easier, comfier life.

● Some inventions are just for fun. The first Frisbees were empty pie tins belonging to a baker called Joseph Frisbie. When some of his customers tossed the tins to each other in the park, the idea for the Frisbee was born.

4

Is everything invented?

● Safety pins were introduced almost 200 years ago, but have a much longer history. Their inventor copied the idea from clasps worn by the Ancient Egyptians.

No it isn't! An invention is something new like a paper-clip, which never existed before someone thought of it. But things like coal and rubber weren't invented. They were already in the world, and just had to be discovered.

● When people first discovered the milky juice of the rubber tree they used it to make rubber. Later, someone invented rubber tyres for cars and bicycles.

Where do inventors get their ideas?

Inventors get ideas for their inventions in lots of different places. Some of them study plants and animals to see how they have solved their problems. Others look at ideas from other places or from the past. Very few ideas come out of the blue.

● Burdock seeds are covered with tiny hooks that stick to things, but can be pulled off. An engineer who noticed this used his discovery to make Velcro for fastenings.

Which new invention was soon on everyone's lips?

In 1915 American scientists came up with a small invention that was a huge success. It was a creamy, colour crayon inside a case that could be wound up and used in a second – the very first lipstick.

● Ancient Egyptian women didn't have wind-up lipsticks, but they did colour their lips. They used golden clay mixed with juicy tree sap.

Who wore a mouthful of hippo teeth?

About 2,500 years ago people began to make false teeth from ivory or bone. Hippo bone was popular, but so was ox, cat and human bone. Unfortunately, all these false teeth soon turned brown and started to rot. They must have tasted dreadful!

- Before lipsticks, lip colours came in a pot. Many of them were waxes and ointments coloured with plant dyes such as grape juice.

- A French hairdresser has used a video camera linked to a computer to show his clients what they would look like with different styles – short hair, long hair, or no hair at all!

Why were plasters first invented?

Earl Dickson invented plasters for his wife, who kept cutting herself in the kitchen. He stuck small squares of cloth on to pieces of sticky tape, covering them carefully to stop the glue drying out. Whenever his wife cut herself, she just grabbed a piece of the tape, and stuck it on.

- Before Mr King Camp Gillette invented safe, modern razors in 1895, men shaved with sharp cut-throat razors – and hoped that their hand wouldn't slip!

Who first flushed the toilet?

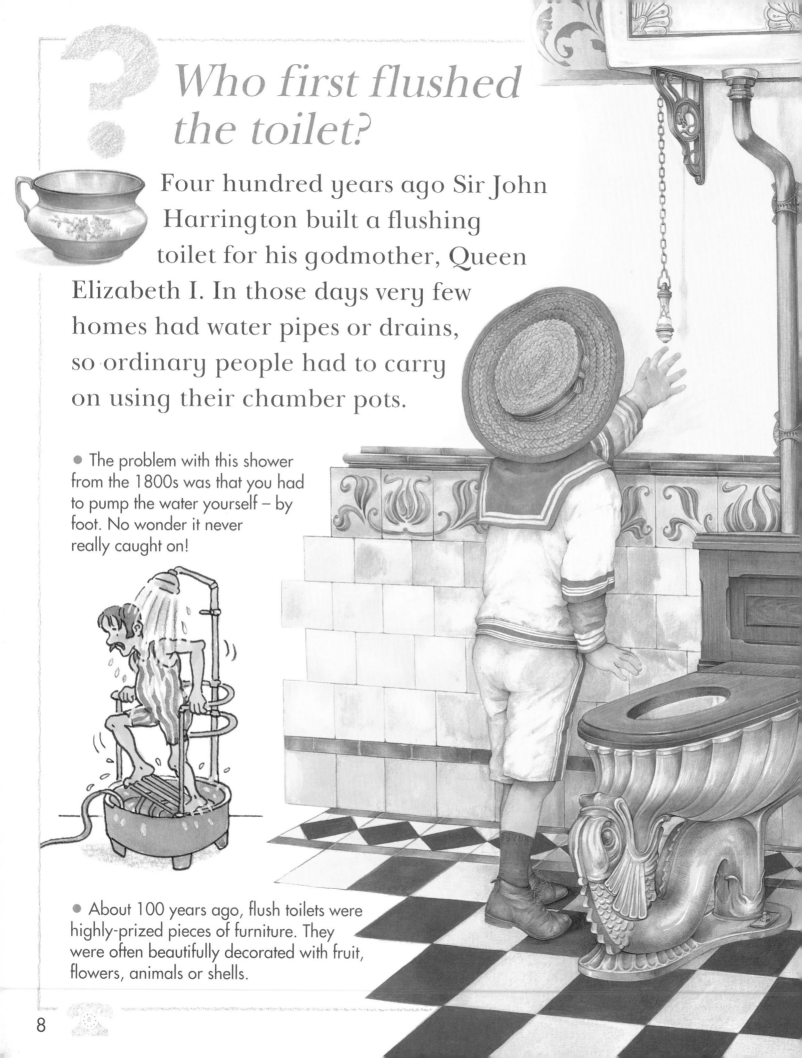

Four hundred years ago Sir John Harrington built a flushing toilet for his godmother, Queen Elizabeth I. In those days very few homes had water pipes or drains, so ordinary people had to carry on using their chamber pots.

● The problem with this shower from the 1800s was that you had to pump the water yourself – by foot. No wonder it never really caught on!

● About 100 years ago, flush toilets were highly-prized pieces of furniture. They were often beautifully decorated with fruit, flowers, animals or shells.

Who first jumped in the bath?

The people of Greece, Rome and the Indus Valley in Pakistan all enjoyed a bath in ancient times. But, as time went by, baths went out of fashion and many people never even washed. They used perfumes to cover up the pong!

● The Chinese used pig's hair to make the first toothbrushes about 500 years ago. Luckily for pigs, nylon brushes came along in the 1930s!

How did horses help keep carpets clean?

The first carpet-cleaning machine was towed by horses! It was parked outside the house because of its smelly petrol engine. Long pipes stretched through the windows and sucked up all the dirt. It was quite a sight and people often invited their friends round to watch!

Who invented raincoats?

● A lot of today's rainwear is made of PVC. It's a plastic-backed material which comes in lots of bright colours.

The first waterproof raincoats were made in 1823 by Charles Macintosh – which is why they are often called macs. He made the cloth waterproof by sandwiching a layer of rubber between two lengths of cotton. The coats kept people dry all right, but they weighed a ton and smelt awful when they got wet!

● It rains so much in Scotland that hill farmers buy raincoats for their sheep!

Why do zips have teeth?

Without their teeth, zips couldn't open or close. The two rows of teeth are joined by a slider, which locks them together or pulls them apart. Zips were invented in the 1890s, and were a great improvement on fiddly buttons and hooks and eyes.

● The first jeans were made by Levi Strauss for gold miners in the USA. He made them in a hard-wearing blue cloth that was used to make tents. These days it's better known as denim.

Can clothes keep you feeling fit?

Some clothes can do amazing things. You can even buy tights full of health-giving vitamins, which are usually only found in fresh fruit and veg!

● When Thomas Hancock invented elastic in 1820, he thought it would be useful along the top of pockets to stop thieves. It was someone else who realized it would be just right for holding up people's underwear!

What did people use before fridges?

Electric fridges were invented around 1920. Before then, people kept their food in a wooden cupboard called an icebox. Huge blocks from the ice man kept the cupboard cold.

● Coca-Cola didn't start out as a fizzy drink. An American chemist called John Pemberton invented it as a sweet syrup in 1885. Soda water was added to it later.

Who ate the first cornflakes?

Two brothers, Will and John Kellogg, invented cornflakes by accident, when they were trying to make a new type of bread. One day, they overcooked a pan of wheat, rolled the mixture flat, and then watched it dry into flakes. They toasted the flakes and tasted them – delicious!

• The ice man called several times a week to deliver large blocks of ice for the icebox.

• Long ago, people made natural fridges by lining caves and holes with a thick layer of snow in winter. These ice houses kept fresh food cool right through the warm summer months.

• In 1853, a new food was invented. When a diner asked for extra-thin chips, the chef came up with the first potato crisps.

How were drinking straws invented?

One hot summer in the 1880s, a man called Marvin Stone made the first paper straw. He'd noticed that people kept drinks cooler by not touching the glass and using a hollow grass stalk to suck up the liquid.

Why are bears called teddies?

Teddy bears are named after the American President, Theodore Roosevelt, who was called Teddy for short. Once, on a hunting trip, he came across a bear cub and refused to shoot it. A sweetshop owner who read about the story in the paper decided to give up his shop and make toy bears. He called them teddies, after the President.

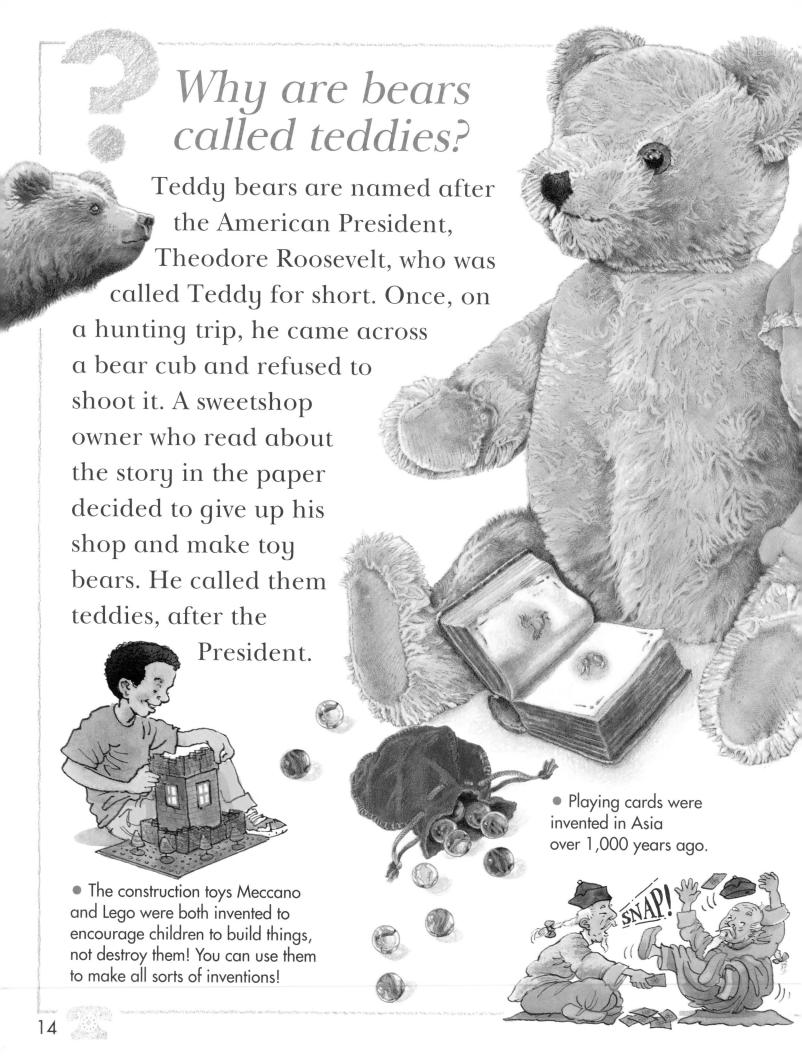

● Playing cards were invented in Asia over 1,000 years ago.

● The construction toys Meccano and Lego were both invented to encourage children to build things, not destroy them! You can use them to make all sorts of inventions!

SNAP!

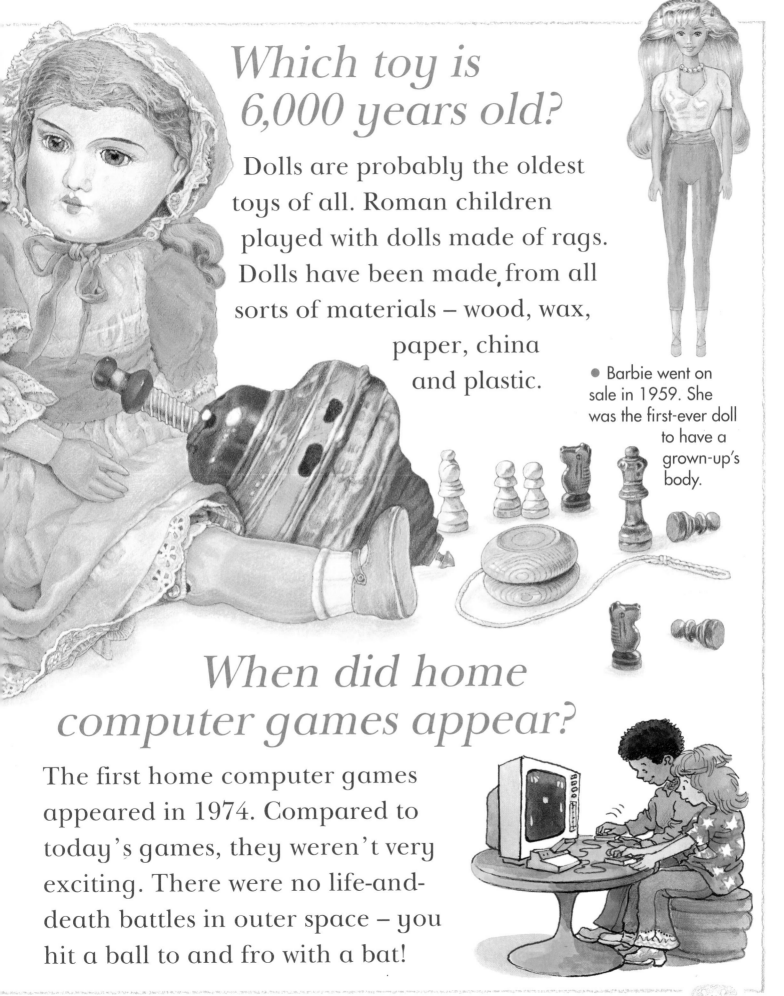

Which toy is 6,000 years old?

Dolls are probably the oldest toys of all. Roman children played with dolls made of rags. Dolls have been made from all sorts of materials – wood, wax, paper, china and plastic.

● Barbie went on sale in 1959. She was the first-ever doll to have a grown-up's body.

When did home computer games appear?

The first home computer games appeared in 1974. Compared to today's games, they weren't very exciting. There were no life-and-death battles in outer space – you hit a ball to and fro with a bat!

15

How do you make toast without a toaster?

People made toast long before there were electric toasters. They put a piece of bread on the end of a long toasting fork, and held it in front of a fire. Unfortunately, the bread burnt easily, and needed very careful watching. The first pop-up toaster was invented in the USA about 70 years ago.

● Electric toasters save us from having to keep an eye on the toast – and from burning it, too!

● In 1937 a new automatic tea-making machine was invented. It heated water, made the tea and then woke you with an alarm. At first it was called the Cheerywake, but it was soon renamed the Teasmade.

Who invented the microwave oven?

Percy Spencer invented the microwave oven just after the Second World War. He'd been working on ways of using invisible waves to detect enemy planes. When the waves melted the chocolate bar in his pocket, he realized they'd be useful for cooking too!

• Microwaves are invisible waves of energy. When they're beamed at food, any water in the food starts to shake violently, and gets very hot. The heat passes quickly through the food, and cooks it all the way through.

• About 100 years ago, only rich people had electricity in their homes. The first electrical gadgets were dangerous things, and servants sometimes risked their lives by using them.

Why don't non-stick frying pans stick?

Non-stick pans don't stick because they are coated with something as slippery as ice, called Teflon. Teflon is actually a kind of plastic, and was invented in the late 1930s. But it took years for someone to come up with the idea of sticking the stuff on to a pan!

Who scored goals in a basket?

The very first basketball players used two old peach baskets as goals. Basketball was invented about 100 years ago by coach James Naismith, who was looking for an exciting game to play indoors on cold winter nights.

Why are trainers so springy?

Trainers have springy soles made of rubber and little pockets of air. Each time you take a step, the rubber gets squashed down, but quickly springs back to its original size. All this squashing and springing makes your feet bounce off the ground, and helps you to run a little bit faster.

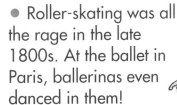

● Roller-skating was all the rage in the late 1800s. At the ballet in Paris, ballerinas even danced in them!

● Early basketball players had to climb a ladder to get the ball back after a goal. Things are easier today – now the goal nets have a hole in the bottom.

How did people ice-skate in summer?

Before there were ice rinks, people could only ice-skate outdoors in the winter. Then someone came up with the idea of making a 'ground' skate that people could enjoy in the summer, too. Instead of a blade, they put wheels on the sole and hey presto – the roller skate had arrived!

● Jet-skis first went on sale in Japan in 1979. Jet-skiers have to steer well clear of bathers. The very latest models can zoom along at speeds of 105 km/h.

What were the first cars like?

The first cars were steam engines on wheels – noisy, smoky machines that scared other road-users! But these steam cars soon got quicker and easier to drive. They were used for nearly 30 years, until they were replaced by faster cars with petrol engines.

● In the 1930s, planes carried 20 passengers at the most. By the 1970s, the new jumbo jets could seat up to 500! Soon, new super-jumbos will carry as many as 850 people!

How do you ride on air?

People ride on air every time they travel on a hovercraft. The hovercraft was invented by Christopher Cockerell in 1959. He discovered that trapping a cushion of air beneath a boat lifts it up above the waves, allowing it to travel much faster.

- The penny-farthing bicycle was invented in the 1860s. It had two wheels – one very large and one very small – and was named after two British coins of the time – the large penny and the tiny farthing.

- Eveyone knows about seat belts for people to wear, but did you know that cats and dogs can wear them too? So clunk-click, Rover/Felix!

- The first cars weren't allowed to go faster than 3 km/h. And someone had to walk in front with a flag to warn other road-users!

Which bikes have sails?

The fastest superbikes have solid wheels and flat frames that work in the same way as a sail. As the bike zooms along, its wheels and frame catch the wind, which helps to push the bike forward – just as it does on a boat. But most of the power still comes from turning the pedals!

How can you fit 1,000 books in your pocket?

There's room for about 1,000 storybooks on a CD-ROM – a small compact disc that's as thin as your fingernail and can fit in a pocket. Words, pictures and sounds can all be stored on CD-ROMs, but they only work with a computer, so you can't read one on the bus – yet!

• The Egyptians were one of the first peoples to write with ink. They made it by mixing black soot with sticky tree sap.

• Just like dinosaurs, the typewriter will soon be extinct. It was a new invention in 1873, but has now been replaced by computers and word-processors.

• Felt-tip pens went on sale in Japan in 1962. Their inventor hoped that the pen's soft tip would make people's handwriting more graceful – like the brushstrokes in Japanese calligraphy.

● Today's pocket calculators can carry out calculations much quicker than you can move your fingers. They are as powerful as the huge computers of the 1960s.

Which computer was as big as a bus?

The first computer was about as long as four buses and was called Colossus. It was built in Britain and was switched on in 1943. Very few people knew about it at the time, because one of its first jobs was to crack secret codes in the war.

Who was Mr Biro?

Ladislao Biro invented the ballpoint pen in 1938. It contained a tube of long-lasting, quick-drying ink, which rolled evenly onto the paper thanks to a tiny ball at the tip. Although Biro called his pen a ballpoint, most people now call their ballpoint a biro!

How did a till settle a row?

In James Ritty's saloon in Ohio, USA, the customers were always arguing with the staff about how much they had to pay for their drinks. So in 1879 Ritty invented a cash register, which rang up the prices, kept a record of how much money was in the till, and gave Ritty and his staff a much more peaceful life.

● Since 1980, goods sold in shops have had a bar code on them. Only a laser scanner can understand the bar code's pattern, which contains all sorts of information about the item.

FOR SALE

Who used tea as money?

People in Tibet and China once used tea pressed into blocks as money. Before coins were invented, people used to swap things like shells, beads or grain for the goods they wanted.

● The Chinese first used paper bank-notes about 1,200 years ago. They printed some of their notes on the bark of the mulberry tree.

How can a supermarket trolley make you rich?

The person who invented the world's first supermarket trolley became a millionaire. Sylvan Goldman's trolley was little more than a chair on wheels, with two baskets fitted on the top, but it earned him a fortune.

● Inventions needn't be grand. When Margaret Knight invented flat-bottomed paper bags, she became a wealthy woman. The bags held twice as much shopping!

Which came first – screws or screwdrivers?

Spiral or twisted nails were used in the 1500s in guns, armour and clocks. But, strangely, you couldn't unscrew a screw for another 300 years, when the handy screwdriver first appeared.

● Today's carpenters use many of the same tools as carpenters long ago.

● Screws weren't made by machine until the 1760s. The thread that runs round the screw had to be filed by hand. That must have been a fiddly task!

Who had everything under lock and key?

The Ancient Egyptians invented locks. Two wooden bolts fitted together snugly and were held in place by pins arranged in a pattern. The pins could only be freed with a key which had a matching pattern.

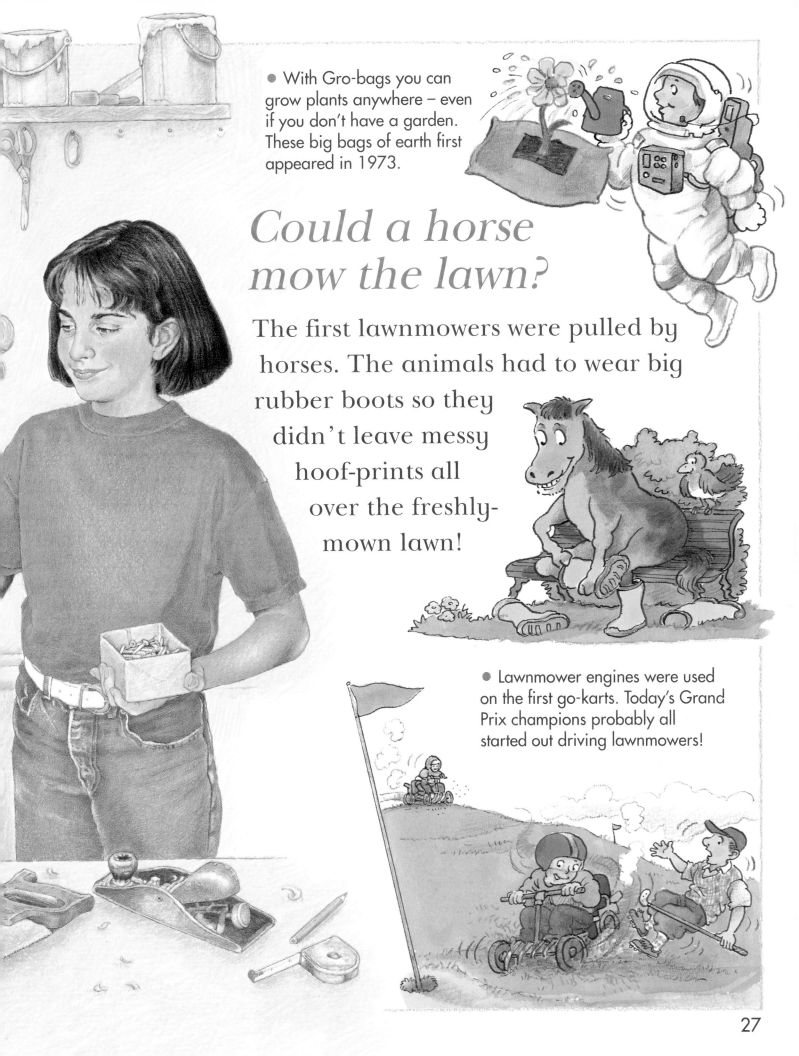

● With Gro-bags you can grow plants anywhere – even if you don't have a garden. These big bags of earth first appeared in 1973.

Could a horse mow the lawn?

The first lawnmowers were pulled by horses. The animals had to wear big rubber boots so they didn't leave messy hoof-prints all over the freshly-mown lawn!

● Lawnmower engines were used on the first go-karts. Today's Grand Prix champions probably all started out driving lawnmowers!

Who took hours to take a photo?

A Frenchman called Joseph Niépce took the first-ever photograph in 1826. He had to wait eight hours before the picture was captured on a thin metal plate coated with a sort of tar. The photo was of the view from his window.

● Niépce would have found it hard to believe, but today's Polaroid cameras can produce a picture in seconds!

● In the late 1800s, it took so long to take a photo that sitters needed a back-rest to help them sit still!

When could you watch pink TV?

The first TV had an odd picture – bright pink and very fuzzy! But its inventor, John Logie Baird, had used very odd equipment to build it, including a bicycle light and a knitting needle!

The world's smallest radio is about the size of a pea!

Who invented the personal stereo?

A Walkman is a personal cassette player with headphones, which is light enough to carry around. It was invented in 1979 by a Japanese electrical company called Sony.

● The first telephone service started in 1878, in a small town in the USA. Only 20 people had phones, so they could only ring up each other!

How can you fight a hungry dinosaur?

When you put on a virtual reality helmet, you enter an imaginary world. You could be fighting a man-eating dinosaur or visiting aliens in space. Everything inside the helmet looks and sounds real, but is actually created by a computer.

● As you press buttons in the special data-glove, the computer changes the pictures you see and the sounds you hear.

● Anyone can be an inventor! What would you like to invent?

• Scientists are experimenting with fruit and vegetables to produce useful, tasty foods. One day they may come up with square tomatoes which you can stack neatly on a shelf.

Are there insects on Mars?

No, but there soon will be! Scientists are building small robots to explore Mars and other planets. The robots have six legs, and look rather like giant insects. They seem to behave like insects too, because they've been programmed to look for food. The food's not for them, though – it's for us, if we ever live on Mars!

• Cars of the future may have a computer on board, which could plan the driver's route. It would even warn drivers of hold-ups on the road ahead, and suggest a good short-cut.

Index